How to be a Better Human

12 Practices for Standing Strong in a Strung-Out World

Jessica Bott

Copyright © 2021 Jessica Bott
Published by The Convoy Group, LLC
PO Box 533051
Orlando, FL 32853

All rights reserved. No part of this publication may be reproduced, stored in a retrieval system, or transmitted in any form or by any means—for example, electronic, photocopy, recording—without prior written permission of the publisher, except as permitted by the 1976 Copyright Act. The only exception is brief quotations in a printed review.

Library of Congress Control Number: 2021900085

ISBN 979-8-5771-6223-8

Cover design by Emma Bush

To my Abba,
Thank you for always leading me into Life,
especially in the most practical, day-to-day ways.
Love You.

CONTENTS

Introduction	1
Practice 1: The Power of Self-Examination	3
Practice 2: The Power of Personal Responsibility	9
Practice 3: The Power of Humility	15
Practice 4: The Power of Brokenheartedness	21
Practice 5: The Power of Forgiveness	27
Practice 6: The Power of Living Without Offense	33
Practice 7: The Power of Sitting in Our Pain	39
Practice 8: The Power of Overcoming	43
Practice 9: The Power of Being With	49
Practice 10: The Power of Telling the Truth	55
Practice 11: The Power of Renewing Your Mind	61
Practice 12: The Power of Generosity	67
Keep Standing	75
Acknowledgements	79
Additional Resources	81

JESSICA BOTT

Introduction

I love the imagery of standing. A friend commented how "standing" means we're choosing in—we're not sitting around or lying about waiting for someone else to do something or awaiting our demise. Standing is an active posture. Standing cultivates strength. Watchmen stand. They stay at the ready at their post, prepared to engage on a moment's notice. I love that picture.

Standing requires something of us. It's sacrificial in the sense that not everyone will choose it, but some of us must. When it comes to living powerfully in this world of ours, so often we look outward regarding what needs to change instead of probing inward. In a strung-out world that's carried to and fro by the latest news cycle, social media post, or personal conversation filled with gossip and slander, will we be the people who look inward and take stock of our personal ugly in order to heal and transform? Will we be the people who say, "Wow, I've got some work to do." Will we be the people who get so very sick of ourselves that we decide to truly be better humans? No one can choose this path for me. No one can choose this path for you.

In the wake of ongoing uncertainty and so many questions about how genuine and helpful change can not only occur but take root, I offer you these 12 powerful practices. Each is not *only* a practice for self-reflection, but something deeper—an invitation to actively stand in both freedom and wholeness in your life.

No matter your circumstances, what you've faced in the past, are wrestling with in the present, or hoping for in the future, I truly believe that when taken to heart and practiced in day-to-day life, these guideposts will lead you well into maturity, depth of character, and ongoing personal transformation.

At least, that's what they've done for me and I'm still, quite literally, practicing. Each and every day. Will you join me?

PRACTICE 1

The Power of Self-Examination

Sitting around the oversized ottoman in our family room, I was headed for internal combustion. The dice rolled, cards were passed out, and trades were made as we played one of our favorite games, *Settlers of Catan*. In our family, when I say "favorite," what I really should say is how we're so crazy about *Settlers* that we have a family trophy. It's made of a glass globe resting atop a glass pedestal, the dark square-shaped base is inscribed, "I'M #1, BOTT FAMILY SETTLERS." While the trophy itself is fairly new to us, it's now annually awarded to the victor of our extended sessions of play. So yes, we're those people.

It was now my dad's turn. He blocked me with the "Robber." And, for whatever reason, I literally went from zero to 60 in about two seconds flat. I don't remember what I said. Isn't that how it goes when one flies into anger-rage? All I remember is the feeling I felt in the wake of my reaction. Just as I was trying to locate what occurred in the aftermath, my sister put words to it: "Wow, that just sucked all of the fun out of the room."

Deep in my belly, I felt it. You might know it—it was like a kettlebell sat inside it. Maybe two. My anger shifted briefly now into shame. Thankfully, I didn't let that stick. Still, I wondered, "Why in the world did I go completely over the edge like that?"

When it comes to taking a good look in the mirror, it's not always fun. But I had to face myself after my outburst. Ever been in that boat?

In the week that followed this moment I took a lot of time for self-examination. Meaning, I took a good look in the mirror and I started asking important questions of myself. (And did some serious apologizing.)

The thing is, there's a legacy of competition I've picked up and I carry it around in my life. My anger in that moment wasn't an isolated event and I think seeing it with fresh eyes (and feeling that heavy pit in my stomach) caused me to pause and make a new decision. Would I choose to dismiss, stuff, or deny its existence again? Or would I deal with it this time?

I chose to deal. I ended up back in some memories from childhood, actually. There was this sort-of unique phrase that came up as I went into my personal discovery process, two words filled with meaning somehow—orphan spirit.

We all probably know that an orphan is someone without a family. They can lack a sense of belonging, being protected, provided for, and feeling safe. Without a home or a supportive family structure, that experience can lead someone to self-protect, compete for affection, attention, and even love.

And even though I grew up in a loving two-parent home, I've had to learn to recognize that there were still gaps in my experience of belonging, being protected, safe, and loved in a meaningful way at times. I just hadn't connected some of those experiences with my need to win at a game (or win in general). Digging in can teach us so much.

At this point, you might be saying or thinking, "Um, isn't that a little deep for getting angry during a game?" If that's you, I can understand how it might seem that way. But the truth is, it is *that deep*, which is the reason I had to get my arms around where it has come from in my life. Because the truth is, as a 42-year-old woman, I'm still operating in some of those gaps and I'm taking it out on the people in my life. And it has to stop.

What about you? What are the seemingly small things in your life that come up over and over again? It could be a consistent pattern, behavior, thought, and/or emotion that leads you into an experience like the one I've shared today. Can you name anything like it?

When it comes to self-examination, certainly we can regularly take stock of ourselves as we grow in self-awareness, but we're often led into the process through our relationships. So today, ask yourself:

- When was the last time I received challenging feedback from someone?

- How did that experience begin? How did it unfold?

- What did I do to process what was shared with me? e.g. received it, dismissed it, blame-shifted, looked into it after-the-fact, etc.

- Did anything change as a result of that experience?

Our willingness to practice self-examination through personal reflection and consideration of the feedback others offer us ensures that we notice how we're showing up in the world. We then get to evaluate if the way we're showing up is congruent with a) who we think we are, and b) who we want to be, and c) how we want others to experience us. Self-examination is powerful because we come out of denial and accept what is true of us right now. Acceptance doesn't mean this is who we'll be or how we'll behave forever, it simply means that we've come to terms with a fact. That fact can then lead us into a change, if we'll let it.

Life's too short to stay stuck in any small or big way in our lives. Being willing to practice self-examination and get to the root of "why" we think, feel, and behave as we do is powerful because it leads us into freedom. We can only control ourselves, so let's take a good look today to see how we can grow, transform, and be the most powerful people on the planet.

Questions for Reflection:

1. What happened this week?

2. How did I react/respond?

3. Why did I react/respond that way?

4. Is there anything I could have done differently? (as I related to myself or to another)

5. What steps can I take now to move forward?

JESSICA BOTT

PRACTICE 2

The Power of Personal Responsibility

Have you ever been in one of those "when it rains, it pours" moments? Just when you think you have enough to work through, another challenge appears on the horizon. For me, it came just as I was beginning to delve into why I went into anger-rage during *Settlers of Catan*. That very same week I found myself on the inside of an unexpected and ugly conflict.

I was on a conference call when my friend, who happened to be the call's facilitator, used a word picture that shocked me. It was as though a dark cloud had fallen over me and I couldn't move forward even though the group dialogue continued. I spoke up within a few minutes and shared how the word picture had affected me. My friend was apologetic and the call seemed to end well.

A day or so later, I received a follow-up email from my friend in which they seemed to be inviting me to look more deeply at why I responded so strongly to their use of that particular word picture. What they didn't know was how I'd actually gotten off the call and spent time processing what I'd been thinking and feeling, so I already knew my "why." I went ahead and responded, sharing what I'd uncovered. It all felt quite benign.

But then I received their next response and somehow, it was no longer benign. Before I knew it, the conversation took a turn and we asked two trusted friends to mediate, helping us to walk through a massive conflict. The end result? The relationship was completely over and I was "cancelled" within a handful of days.

So here I was working through the experience I'd just had with my family and now, a friendship ended without warning. I felt so angry and hurt in the wake of some of the things my friend said to me, but ultimately, I felt heartbroken about losing my friend. My head was spinning and I wondered, "What in the world just happened?"

In both cases, I made a decision to look in the mirror. If you read my account in the last chapter, you already know how I began to move forward regarding my family. When it came to my friend, the bottom line for me was that I simply found their word picture to be very inappropriate and harmful. Through the ensuing communications, my friend went on to tell me how I had deeper work to do in my life. I knew I'd done that work but I made a decision to go further. I asked the mediators to weigh in—did they believe I had more personal work to do? Their response was that I did not. That was helpful and, of course, good to hear in the midst of the hardship.

Now I could have stopped there, but I didn't. You might wonder, "Why wouldn't you stop there??" And, that's a great question.

During the past decade, in particular, I've found myself delving deeply into the work of personal responsibility. I've been learning to ask more questions as I examine myself and evaluate how I'm showing up in the world. It's not particularly fun work. It's certainly not easy. But, I'm finding that it truly is the path into integrity and personal transformation.

When I say integrity, I mean: who I think that I am and say that I am is actually who I am in my beliefs, thoughts, emotions, behaviors, and wait for it, *motives*. When I say personal transformation, I mean: the ongoing process of becoming and being the very best version of me through healing and personal character (which certainly has everything to do with my integrity). Through personal responsibility, I've learned to ask, "What is my part in this situation?" And this is why I could not stop there.

As I looked back through the written communications, I realized a number of realities:

- Why didn't I pick up the phone and call my friend? Why in the world did I leave the conversation in email? I actually know better than that. The truth is, I remembered how I'd briefly considered calling them but I was afraid. The conversation was already turning ugly. I ran away by staying "safely" behind my computer screen.

- When they seemed to have reacted to one of the items I shared, why didn't I pause and consider, "What did that trigger inside of them?" I literally could see where the change happened in the dialogue. I was so entrenched in the back-and-forth that I missed an opportunity to better care for my friend. Why didn't I just ask them what they heard me saying there?

- I've learned to use my voice again to bring attention to things that cause harm, and to be vulnerable with others. It was good for me to share how I thought my friend's word picture was very inappropriate and harmful. It was good for me to share more of my story with them and why it mattered to me that the language used be more thoughtfully considered. I'm proud of myself for not shrinking back or shutting down but being willing to face conflict and with it, the possibility of rejection, and stay the course. That's still new for me.

- I felt grateful to be able to celebrate a place where I can see growth in my journey. (I think that's important to share with you today because personal responsibility means we also notice how we're living into who we say we are and who we want to be—it's a joy to see when we're living into integrity.)

In the aftermath of being cancelled, I shared what I uncovered above with one of the mediators, and she agreed. Regarding the first two, she told me how it was good for me to see how I could have shifted the dialogue and showed up differently. She said, "Next time!" All of that feedback was good for me to hear. And truth be told, I'm still so sad about this loss. But I've learned a whole lot through it.

As an aside: Do you have friends who will tell you the truth and love you through the challenging places? It makes taking personal responsibility much simpler and it helps when you're walking through a difficulty like this one. It's like finding treasure in this life.

When we take responsibility for ourselves, we set ourselves up to see lasting change in our relationships and even in the way we approach circumstances, no matter the result. When we look in the mirror in self-examination, go deep into considering how we showed up in a given conversation or circumstance, and decide to forgo finger-pointing, we gain personal freedom. This is a powerful way to live.

Questions for Reflection:

1. What happened in the situation?

2. How did I react/respond?

3. Is there anything I could have done differently? (with myself or others)

4. Which part or parts are mine to own?

5. What amends must I make?

JESSICA BOTT

PRACTICE 3

The Power of Humility

My moment had arrived. The other girls in my second-grade class and I were called to center stage. Each of us were ready to demonstrate our ability to perform the dance steps we'd been taught only a few minutes before. Earlier that morning, I'd seen this *gorgeous* costume on one of the racks and asked a nearby teacher which group would get to wear "that one." Our school was celebrating Cinco De Mayo and the costume in question was green, white, and red. It had these wonderful layered ruffles and the top of the dress sat slightly off the shoulder. My eyes were filled with shooting stars as I imagined myself looking just so beautiful in it. I loved looking beautiful, after all. Hehe.

It just so happened, one particular dance number was tied to the opportunity to wear the coveted costume, so my attention turned to learning and becoming *a-mazing* at those dance moves so I would be chosen to be in that group. The thing is, to this day I don't really have the greatest rhythm, but my little seven-year-old self was convinced she could do it and that her whole life would be made in that moment.

Unfortunately, as I stood alongside the other girls and performed, the teacher in charge of the performance didn't see my potential. In fact, she was cruel to me personally, telling me how bad I was at the steps before dismissing me from the stage. I ran to the back of our school auditorium and cried and cried.

Oh, life. For seven-year-old me, this was a lot of loss. And the experience shaped me.

In my mid-thirties, I took some time to revisit this memory. I was in a season of healing and in a time of prayer with two other people, when I felt invited to ask God where He was in that memory. As I did, I was right back at seven again.

I was running from that stage, up the aisle between the wooden auditorium chairs, and, as I fell onto the ground behind the last row, I cried. This time was different, though. I looked up. And when I did, He was standing there. I felt compelled to go over to Him and He hugged me for a long while, then He wiped my tears away. The next thing surprised me the most: He kneeled down and looked me in the eyes and said, "Jessica, I have a different role for you to play in this production. I've made you to be an encourager and so I want you to get back in there and celebrate each and every person on that stage." I nodded, took a deep breath, and felt excitement rise within me. I hugged Him again, now smiling broadly, before running down that aisle and back onto the stage where I proceeded to find something wonderful about each person I came across. I shared what I saw with them and in some cases, I simply cheered someone on. It felt awesome. I felt so special. I loved seeing my fellow students through new eyes and it was so sweet to see how encouraged they were by what I noticed and shared with them. I didn't care about the cruel words spoken to me or that gorgeous costume anymore. There were more important things to give my attention to now.

Coming out of that prayer experience, something profoundly shifted in me. For so many years I'd seen myself as "one-down" because of my inability to perform well and unfortunately, as a result of that teacher's unkindness to me. In fact, over the years since, I had a pattern of pursuing only the activities I knew I could succeed in to some measure. I became pretty calculated and concerned myself with my own competence.

None of this was conscious, of course. So often, we make agreements as children that we don't remember, but they affect us until they're seen and dealt with later in life. Instead of originally experiencing a bit of humility, gaining a proper perspective of myself and others, and accepting that I just wasn't great at those steps, what I actually encountered and took on was humiliation, a friend of shame. And I never wanted to feel like that again.

Earlier I shared that humility is about having a proper perspective of ourselves, but I also value this definition from the online Cambridge Dictionary: *The feeling or attitude that you have no special importance that makes you **better than** others.* (We can interchange *less than*, as well.) In that prayer time, I got in touch with how I was made special and when I operated out of my uniqueness, it was truly something remarkable. After that experience, I thought differently of myself and was actually freed up from a lot of baggage and bad behavior.

Even though people in my life might not have always seen it, I lived so many years deeply insecure and consumed with myself. Those two realities go hand in hand. Insecurity has this way of ensuring our focus is always on us. I put myself down through comparison. In false-humility, I didn't use my voice and/or regularly diminished the value of my contribution as I put others above me—way, way above me. I regularly wondered about what I said, how I said it, how I behaved, and if people were going to accept or reject me. It was a me-me-me focused life and it was exhausting.

In outright arrogance, I always felt like I had something to prove to ensure people knew I was worthwhile, that my life mattered, and for myself, that I was okay. So, I postured myself as knowing it all, having the answer, and made sure I would always be needed. Of course, this also stemmed from insecurity. It just took on a different type of form and attitude. I tried to be more valuable than others by working long hours, coming up with the solution that would be accepted as best, and taking on more than was good for me to handle. I was petrified that people would find out that I might not be as good at something as I presented myself to be, and I worried that someone more naturally talented in an arena I was in might take all of the attention away from me. I was terrified of either being passed up or dispensable or both. And I was a master at positioning myself in what I was good at to hide the internal chaos I felt every day.

In both cases, I was feeding something inside me that was never ever satiated. And in genuine transparency, there are days when these postures still rear their ugly heads. Which is why living in humility is so powerful because it gives us tracks to run on when ugly or old patterns try to retain or regain ground in our lives.

<hr>

When it comes to the practice of humility, having a proper view of ourselves and others frees us up to:

- See and celebrate our strengths and keep on growing as we make our good contribution in the world. We see ourselves properly and get excited to give!

- See and celebrate the strengths of others and marvel at their good contribution in the world. We stop competing and comparing and we start working together.

- Self-examine regularly to understand our beliefs and motives so we continue to live in humility, not putting ourselves above or below another.

- Take personal responsibility for what is ours to own as we engage ourselves and those in our paths, even when that means owning where our lack of humility comes from in the first place.

Practicing humility produces powerful outcomes. Let's dig deeper.

Questions for Reflection:

1. How am I doing in the area of humility?

2. What are my greatest hang-ups in viewing myself and others properly?

3. Where do those hang-ups come from?

4. What will I do about it now?

JESSICA BOTT

PRACTICE 4

The Power of Brokenheartedness

It was Valentine's Day 1989 and the two fifth grade classes were in motion between both classrooms, handing out cards and candy to one another. The night before, I'd made a decision. Earlier that week a boy in my class gave me a gift on the bus ride home before he got off at his stop. The earrings had large clear stones and we all thought they must be diamonds. One of the other boys later "tested" them out to see if they were real—we were all convinced they were. The necklace was very sweet with a tiny pink stone heart hanging from a gold chain. But I didn't particularly like the boy who gave these gifts to me, especially not in *that* way. He was often unkempt, but he was also bright-eyed, very sweet, and well-meaning. Our families even went to church together, but I wasn't wanting his attention.

So, on Valentine's Day and in the midst of all of the bustle, I marched over to where he was sitting behind his desk, looked him in the eyes and placed his card and gifts on his desk. "I don't want to be your friend anymore," I announced, and turned on my heels and left.

At the time, I remember feeling an uneasiness in my belly as I put my plan in motion, but I dismissed it because I really didn't want his attention. It wasn't normal for me to be so directly unkind to my peers, I usually was the one standing up for those on the edges of the social circle even at a young age. I determined not to let my actions bother me, though his face fell, and I could see that I'd hurt him.

Throughout the rest of my school years and into my adulthood I've often thought about that boy. As I've uncovered pieces of pain from my childhood and experienced more harm along my life's journey, I've wondered if he carried my cruelty with him over the years. I've felt heartbroken about it, actually. I was so unkind, and not just that, but I did it all very intentionally. Even to this day, I feel grief about my actions and regret them. Please hear this, though: I'm not living under a cloud of grief or regret anymore. I've done the work to forgive myself along the way, but I do look back on what I did to that sweet, well-meaning boy and it motivates me to do better to this day.

I wish I could tell you that this story was the last time I did something cruel, but unfortunately it's not. My life story has many markers of times I've gossiped, slandered, acted hatefully, thought horrible thoughts about others, failed to help others when I could have, diminished and dismissed others in efforts to feel secure or keep control, and so much more. The more in touch I stay with the ways I've caused or even desired harm to come to others (through both my actions, or lack thereof, and my thoughts), the more my heart has remained soft.

It's pretty easy to focus on the ways other people have caused harm to us. We can feel justified in both our pain and our unwillingness to release it over time. If you're like me, perhaps you've spent time ruminating on what has been done to you over the years. But how often do we revisit the ways we have harmed others?

I'm convinced that when we live in a posture of brokenheartedness, we all do better by one another in this world. A brokenhearted person is someone who is "overwhelmed by grief or disappointment" (Oxford Lexico online), or "overwhelmed by grief or despair" (Merriam-Webster online). It's a place we get into when we acknowledge, "Wow, I did *that* ..." We don't stay there forever in the sense of being overwhelmed by what we've done for the rest of our lives, but we do take it to heart, and we take it very seriously.

Imagine with me a world in which each one of us feels this type of grief over our harmful thoughts and actions. What if we sat with the things we've done to others, or failed to do, and really understood the harm we've caused? How might we approach our own pain differently? How might our compassion and humility grow?

Being heartbroken by what we've done directly correlates to humility. We cannot be a brokenhearted person if we cannot see ourselves properly, which means we can't genuinely change or transform if we're unwilling to see how we've harmed others and then do something about it. A sense of entitlement will keep us from both brokenheartedness and humility, so we must live aware.

Entitlement says things like:

- I've been harmed, so I'm entitled to hold onto and act out of my pain for as long as I want to.

- What I've done to others isn't nearly as bad as all of the ways I've been harmed by others.

- You shouldn't be upset with me, I didn't mean to _____.

- It's okay for me to _____. Other people do that or have done that to me.

Without an understanding of how our thoughts, words, and actions (including our sense of entitlement and living with a hard-hearted posture) impact those around us, it can be a challenge for us to remain in a brokenhearted posture and live in humility. Growing deeper in character means we grieve well over both what has been done to us and what we have done to others. I truly believe our decision to grow in this area is one of the most powerful catalysts to seeing genuine and lasting change not only in our own lives but also in society.

To be softened to the point that you remain tenderhearted and compassionate toward another, no matter the circumstance, is a thing of beauty. Brokenheartedness cultivates this reality in our lives. Who's ready to live like this?

Questions for Reflection:

Regarding others:

1. On a scale of 1-10, how aware have I been of the ways others have caused harm to me?

2. Have I ruminated on that harm over time? If so, which aspects?

3. Do I notice any patterns in what I ruminate over?

4. What have the results been in my life?

Regarding yourself:

1. On a scale of 1-10, how aware have I been of the ways I have caused harm to others?

2. Have I ruminated on that harm over time? If so, which aspects specifically?

3. Do I notice any patterns in what I ruminate over?

4. What have the results been in my life?

5. What tends to motivate me to make a change? What is typically the decision point or the thing that moves me into action? (e.g. Someone I care for is mad at me and I need to make that better, I'll lose something if I don't change, I change because I can be better than this, etc.)

JESSICA BOTT

PRACTICE 5

The Power of Forgiveness

It was early morning and I was sitting in my car about to pull out of my parking space when my friend of many years, who also happened to be one of my business advisors and current boss, pulled up abruptly. I'd been sick over the weekend and was on my way home to bed after getting into the office for a short time that Monday to put some items in order for the day ahead. We'd been working together for an extended season and in the weeks leading up to this moment, the stress and the challenges in our interactions were so intense that my body was finally giving way. Through my passenger window, I was told that my services were no longer needed and just like that, it was done.

Later that week, a number of emails were exchanged in order to iron out the last pieces of the partnership. In the parking lot, my friend had communicated all was well and that we would talk soon—the emails communicated very differently. I soon realized that all personal and professional ties were ended, which left me feeling so disillusioned, angry, sad, and all of the other emotions that go with grief.

A couple months passed and I sent a personal letter seeking understanding and reconciliation in our relationship. I felt hopeful that maybe repair could happen, yet I never received a response to my letter. Another four months passed and I finally reached a place of acceptance. The relationship in all capacities was over and it was time for me to live like it. It was heartbreaking.

As I hope you can imagine, this is a very clean retelling of a profoundly painful experience and season of grief. My sense of justice regarding how everything went down rose up within me too many times to count. Promises were broken. Accusations were made. I learned about leading statements that were shared and left open in such a way that assumptions were made about me and my departure (I didn't seek this information out, I feel that's important to share). The attempts that I made to pursue reconciliation were ignored. And the wrestling I did regarding forgiveness hit deep places inside of me.

One theme of experience throughout the course of my life is betrayal. So when I was walking through this season, all of the old stories reared their ugly heads. Isn't that how it goes, though? As I had been in the past, I was tempted to hold onto resentment, tempted to go after them in some capacity to let the pain I felt be known, but every time I started to adjust course in that direction, I felt compelled to stop. While I didn't do this process perfectly, I did find myself regularly confronted by these questions: What good would that do? What wrong would my choice to do wrong correct? To what end and for what purpose do I need to do anything further?

We've all likely heard this or a similar metaphor: unforgiveness is like a prison you first put yourself into, lock the door, and then throw away the key. I had a choice to make. Would I live in a posture of unforgiveness or would I forgive my friend whom, despite it all, I loved deeply? Would I cultivate space for my heart to stay soft or would I grow hardened and cold, locking parts of myself away in a horrible prison of my own making?

I chose forgiveness. I chose to remain soft-hearted. I chose to remain in a posture of hope. Was it painless? No. Has it kept me living in freedom? Yes.

If we look around our lives and out into society, it often seems that both individually and collectively we have grown accustomed to holding onto resentment or seeking vengeance instead of fighting against both. The truth is that if we don't choose to operate in forgiveness personally, there is no area, segment, or group within our society currently plagued by vengeance and resentment that will have any hope to experience lasting change. If we don't practice forgiveness personally, how will it ever translate "out there?"

It's not easy. Nothing I'm sharing in this book is easy. These practices, these postures, they require something of us. And sometimes, as in the case of genuine forgiveness, it requires a lot. How many times do we forgive when the same thought or emotion occurs *again* regarding what that person or that group has done to us? My answer? Every single time. I cannot afford to be taken out by a lack of forgiveness, and I propose to you today that you cannot afford it either. Too much is at stake.

When we regularly operate from humility and brokenheartedness, as we talked about in the last chapters, it makes forgiveness a lot simpler. When we do the work of looking in the mirror, when we remember times we have caused harm, when we even remember times we've received forgiveness from someone in a way that shaped our story for the better, then we can forgive. We can forgive again and again and again.

Does our forgiveness excuse the wrong? Not in any way. It simply keeps us out of jail and thereby, able to continue making our best contribution in the world.

Forgiveness also helps us to stay in hope. To this day, I still hope for reconciliation in and restoration of that relationship. I'm not saying we all have to hope for that same outcome, of course. I suppose I just want you to know that it is an option. We can hold hope for both as we heal and as life moves forward. But the bottom line? Forgiveness must be initiated by you and by me. That's how things change for us and in the world, too.

Forgiveness frees us into such a sweeter, lovelier, and healthier life. I invite you to grab a favorite beverage today or sometime this week, get into a quiet place, and make time to consider and write out your responses to the following questions:

1. Is there someone in or around my life who harmed me and as a result, I'm still holding resentment toward them or seeking vengeance for the harm they've caused? If so, who is it?

2. What would it mean for me to forgive them, to release myself from the harm they've caused me through forgiveness?*

3. Will I choose to forgive them today?

Sometimes, we're the ones who need forgiveness. We might be walking around holding something we've done or said, or failed to do, against ourselves. The result? Prison! So please consider:

1. Are there any areas of my life where I haven't forgiven myself? If so, write them out:

2. What would it mean for me to forgive myself, to release myself from the harm I've experienced because of something I've done, something I "should have" known better about, something I didn't do but was supposed to do, etc?*

3. Will I choose to forgive myself today?

*Hint: Imagine your life without you holding onto what you've experienced— what looks, sounds, and feels different in your life? What changes?

It can be powerful, even life-changing, to speak our forgiveness aloud. You can literally state:

"I forgive _____ for
_____."

Get specific. Make a whole list if needed, then speak it all out at once, line-by-line. Let's not live one more day trapped in a prison of unforgiveness.

JESSICA BOTT

PRACTICE 6

The Power of Living Without Offense

Calling the tire store, I found I had a decision to make. They'd assured me a few days before that once my tires were in, they'd call to schedule a time for the installation. Well, a few days had passed and no call. I wondered if they'd ordered them. I wondered if the tires had come in. I wondered if they had come in and if the store had installed them on someone else's vehicle. I spent *plenty* of time wondering. As I picked up the phone to call, I realized I'd worked myself up a bit in all of my wonderings (shocking!). It was slight, but it was there. I also realized I could carry the offense of their lack of communication into that call OR I could release it and simply call to see what was happening with my tires.

If you're thinking, "Sheesh, analytical much?!" Yes, much. Plus, you'll notice how I squandered valuable energy in my wonderings to boot! And, I'm sure *you'd never* do anything like it … But I definitely do! I'm practicing, remember?

One of the ways I regularly notice myself taking offense is in the arena of lack of good communication. It might seem like a small thing, but I hope you'll see how quickly I was moving into full-blown, "Where are my tires?!" and "Why didn't you tell me?!" offense. But because (thank God!) I noticed where I was headed, I was able to make a new decision and make that phone call from a place of peace.

By the way, when I did get the representative on the phone, I went ahead and mentioned how I hadn't received a call from them BUT I did so from a place of curiosity and kindness instead of a place of irritation and annoyance. It's okay to let the fact be the fact. They initiated an apology about their lack of follow-up, found that my tires were in, and scheduled an appointment for the installation. It was all good. (Any other business owners out there find customer feedback helpful? This is why I try to do this in an honorable way once I work through *my* issues.)

Taking offense often starts small and grows from there. We might not even notice how we're subtly taking on offense on a given day and how we become so accustomed to being offended that we just live like that all of the time, in the small and in the great. I could share so very many examples of my ongoing work in this area. The truth is, when we don't notice, we keep walking in it. Sometimes we even pick up offenses that don't belong to us.

Say a loved one comes to you and shares a story about something that happened at work or in the family or on the road or in the grocery line that day? So often, we don't stay neutral. In our desire to help them to feel better or heard, we pick up the offense and run with it. We do this in so many ways—getting on the gossip train and retelling the tale to anyone who will listen, looking the person up on social media and pointing out everything wrong with them as a human being, or taking on anger or judgement within ourselves by thinking we're somehow better than they are, like "I'd never! ..." The examples seem inexhaustible.

Being offended is a choice. Whether we realize it or not, we make a rapid-fire decision to take it on and walk it out. In the same way, we can make a decision to notice the warning signs, see what's building inside of us, and stop it in its tracks.

Like my example, I've learned some of the areas where I quickly move into offense relate to a lack of communication. Another is when I encounter or notice injustice. It's hard for me to remain neutral at times, so I must be aware. Yet another way I can make a rapid-fire decision to be offended is when I'm misunderstood, or my intentions are questioned. I've definitely been offended by someone taking offense like, "I'm so offended that you're offended by the thing I said or did…!!" That's all so lovely, right?

—————

Can you imagine waking up and living an entire day without being offended? I mean, really think about it. Think of yesterday or earlier today. Where did you find yourself moving toward or engaging in a practice of offense?

Go further, imagine an entire world of human beings who refuse to take offense. I mean, the kind of humans who get on social media or watch the news or have an actual conversation or interaction with another person and will not take on offense from anything they see, hear, or experience. What would that even look like? Per normal, it starts with you and with me.

When we begin to take notice and take steps to not be offended, 1) we can stay better connected in relationships while avoiding disunity; 2) we get to look deeper and ask: what else is going on with me or with the other person? 3) we continue to live in a posture of humility; and 4) we live empowered to bring resolution, understanding, and wisdom into circumstances and situations. Plus, we don't waste valuable energy like I did by spinning around asking questions that a simple phone call would answer. (I'm choosing to celebrate that hiccup as growth!)

Let me be clear and say, the decision not to be offended does not mean that:

- We accept everything as good and right.

- We don't take action to address realities that are wrong in our world.

It does mean, however, that we live freely and lightly in our minds and hearts. We stay in peace. We keep our cool. We stay connected to the best of our ability (we can only control ourselves, after all). We employ our energy to create solutions. We don't get sidetracked by the minors when the majors are right in front of our faces. Imagine the problems we could solve if you and I used our time, energy, and resources freed up from offense! Now that's something to go after...

It's truly powerful to live without offense. Won't you join me? We can do this by staying on top of our thoughts, emotions, and behaviors that keep us connected to picking up and running with an offense.

Together, let's go after greater levels of freedom!

Questions for Reflection:

1. Where am I living offended?

2. What are some patterns I notice about being offended or taking offense?

3. What are some areas of life or topics of conversation that stir up feelings of offense in me? (e.g. irritation, annoyance, resentful displeasure, etc)

4. Where am I picking up an offense that doesn't even belong to me?

5. What am I willing to do about it?

JESSICA BOTT

PRACTICE 7

The Power of Sitting in Our Pain

It was 2009 and I'd just relocated to Florida, temporarily, or so I'd thought. My overarching experience of my life could be captured in one word—numb. I'd taken on an interim role for 10 months to escape another year in Boston, a city I loved but couldn't seem to thrive in. Everything felt hard but I'd been working and working and working trying to prove myself while avoiding the feelings of how bad it felt to be me in my life.

Within the first few weeks of life in Orlando, I slowly allowed myself to get out to enjoy the area and figure out what life could look like without work at the center. But things rapidly changed when I contracted the swine flu and spent the next five weeks mostly out of the office, feeling horrible physically, isolated relationally, and didn't have a single item to distract me from the pain that started to surface within me.

The truth is, I was deeply in debt, experiencing strain in family and personal relationships, had put on 20+ pounds, felt absolutely directionless and disappointed in my vocational life, and felt overlooked and not known by those whom I thought did know me.

And I just had to sit in it. During every waking hour, I was confronted with pain and could do nothing to push it back into some neat little closet. It was the worst time for weeks and weeks, but then it somehow became the absolute best.

What I was most afraid of in that season was that if unleashed, my pain would overwhelm me and that'd be it. I wouldn't recover as a human. Somehow, I reasoned it was better to stuff, deny, and avoid because then I wouldn't lose control. But the truth is, I'd already lost control. I'd given myself over to workaholism, I was in financial distress, my body was suffering, my self-image was super low, and I felt all-around lost. All of my efforts to hold onto a semblance of control were failing me. I finally reached acceptance. And when that gave, life started to come back to me.

So often these days, I find I'm not alone in the way I've approached pain. Each of us tends to deny, run away from, or "get over" our pain in some capacity while never really dealing with it. The thing is, when we don't deal with it, we can't get over it. It shows up in the lies we believe, our words, in the way we behave toward ourselves and others, in our bodies through exhaustion, sickness, disease, and more. It doesn't leave us. It takes hold of us one way or another. And when we're gripped by realities that lend more toward death, how can we expect life in return?

It's all well and good to talk about the power of sitting in our pain, but what does that actually involve? How does life get to find its way back to us? What does that even mean?

For me, it's looked a lot like:

- Identifying the painful, hard, and/or challenging places in my life right now.

- Capturing why that's hard—noting what I think about or feel when I think on that reality.

- Noticing the behaviors that follow this line of thinking and/or feeling that aren't helping me right now.

- Asking: what is the actual truth about this thing in my life? It's okay if you don't know right away, you can acknowledge it and even write, "I don't know the truth about _____ right now."

- Then, noticing again: how does all of the above feel now that I've acknowledged it?

I've learned to give myself permission not to figure out what to do with painful, hard, or challenging pieces that come up in this process because, often, I don't know. I simply need to allow myself the space to process that it's real, acknowledge the kind of effect it's having on me, and see if I can sort out the truth about a) where it's come from, b) why it is so painful, hard, and/or challenging, and c) what I believe about myself because that thing exists in my life right now. It's a form of grieving.

Sitting in our pain is so much more about acknowledgement than fixing. Fixing comes later. For such a long time I didn't know that, though. I didn't know I could simply acknowledge and trust that in the process of acknowledgement, the solution would still come.

I also didn't know that I could acknowledge without falling into the trap of victimhood. It took me a long while to learn that a victim mentality isn't born of noticing and acknowledging pain, but rather it's born from staying in it, never finding the exit once it's felt and acknowledged.

Today, I invite you to walk through the process of acknowledgment that I've just shared and take notice of your pain, your hardships, and your challenges. Set aside some time where you can be present in the process. If you're a person of faith, invite God to meet you and go through it together. Ask what He'd like to say to you about the items that come up for you.

I love this process because it really does "take a load off," in the truest form of that phrase. And, it's okay if you have an emotional response. When we willingly look at our pain, it can take some time to adjust to being that present with ourselves and our thoughts and/or feelings. Please allow yourself the freedom to be exactly where you are in the moment and show yourself kindness whether emotions arise or not.

And, please remember ... In order to get over it, we must move through it. In order to move through it, we must be willing to sit in it. If we don't sit in it and grieve it, we'll *always* live with it in one way or another.

HOW TO BE A BETTER HUMAN

PRACTICE 8

The Power of Overcoming

Way back in the 12th grade, I enrolled in two advanced placement (AP) courses offered by my high school: AP Literature and AP US History. My goal was to challenge myself academically and also to gain college credit at year-end by taking the AP exams (saving cash and avoiding some general education coursework in college sounded good to me!).

Yet when it came to getting that college credit I had to score a three, four, or five on the exam. A one or two would only gift me a "thanks for participating" nod. During our mock-AP exams that winter, I scored well in AP History but my AP Lit score was a dreaded two. I was beside myself. I'd worked so hard in that class and, challenging as it was, I really enjoyed it. Would I really go through all of that effort only to get a participation-pat-on-the-back?

My teacher was tough and she expected a lot from her students. When my score came back she graciously offered to help me—she wanted me to succeed. I could have turned her down. I could have decided the two was the end of my story. But honestly, knowing that she believed I could be and do more made all the difference. I agreed to the help and faithfully met with her for weeks and weeks in order to grow.

When exam time came, I felt confident and encouraged. Weeks later, I received my official AP exam scores in the mail and opened the envelope with cautious optimism. I almost fell over when I read my AP Lit score, a FOUR! I cried in amazement and joy.

My teacher was hosting a post-graduation celebration for our class at her home that week, so I waited to tell her the news. That day, she approached me first and shared, "I received the scores by mail and couldn't wait to read them, so I opened them right here in the foyer."

She went on, "When I came to your score, I screamed so loudly and jumped up and down!! I'm SO PROUD of you!!" She then shared how it was one of her proudest moments because she, always honest, expected a three. The four just blew her expectations out of the water. Now we were both in tears.

Looking back, I know that my decision to overcome paired with her help is what made all the difference. I could have sat in my pain and failure forever, but I would have missed the beauty and power of overcoming. I'm so glad I didn't miss it.

Moments like these shape us. When I'd run into challenges in college, during my first job, dealing with financial stress, moving to a new city, you name it, I could look back at one of my life's markers like this one and keep going. I could tap into that memory, that experience of making it through, doing the work, getting the help, and learning what life looked like on the other side of that opportunity. Then, I could persevere through whatever I was facing knowing it was a powerful decision to stay the course.

Overcoming is all about moving forward. We don't ignore the challenge. We don't pretend like everything's okay. No, we acknowledge and move through the pain so we can start fresh from that new place.

Overcoming is all about solutions, figuring out how to move forward, and then doing it. It will require practice. Often, we need help. A friend, a colleague, a coach, a mentor, an expert in a particular field—we determine the sort of help we need and we ask for help! The first solution we try might not be the thing that brings resolution, but we learn and keep going.

Overcomers make statements like:

- This is not the end of my story.

- This doesn't have to be the end result of this circumstance in my life.

- This doesn't have to be the end of how relationships go in my life.

- I can overcome and do something new, walk in something different, and pursue better.

- I will show up, I will keep going, I will see this through!

I honestly felt a little sheepish about publishing this particular story because, as I'm sure you might assume, I've faced much harder challenges since AP Lit in high school. But the more I thought about why I was sharing it, the better I understood. Quite simply ...

Remembering how I persisted as a 17-year-old deeply encouraged me. It was within me back then, before I knew all that I now know about myself and the world, to try. It was within me to ask for help. When faced with failure, it was within me to devote myself to a process to dig deep and grow into someone more. It was within me to receive feedback throughout the process and take it to heart; that feedback helped me to transform.

When I go back into this memory, I see this lovely glimmer of someone I was becoming. I see what I was really made of back then and it still helps me to know who I am to this day. So, I wonder: what are you made of?

––––––––––

Please hear this from me today … You are so very capable of overcoming, no matter what has happened, no matter what has been done to you, no matter what you have done in your life, decisions you've made that have had negative consequences, you have the ability to make decisions today to overcome. You can gain mastery over that which has tried to master you.

Overcoming is a powerful, powerful decision because it:

- Destroys the victim mentality in our lives that keeps us from taking new ground.

- Develops perseverance and character in us.

- Establishes hope in us. What we have faced doesn't have the last word.

- Cultivates ongoing momentum in our lives for change and transformation.

You and I don't have to stay where we're at today. We can move forward and we can do so in hope and in health. What area of your life could use a good dose of overcoming right now? Your decision to move forward, paired with some help, could be just the thing you need to succeed.

Remember a time when you overcame a difficulty, challenge, sickness, etc., and ask:

1. What did it feel like to overcome?

2. What did it take for me to overcome? Name the specific steps taken to overcome.

3. How did it feel to make it to the other side of what I faced?

4. Did anything change (in my mindset, in the way I behaved, in how I related to myself or others)?

5. Why is that memory meaningful to me today?

JESSICA BOTT

PRACTICE 9

The Power of Being With

Leaving a small group gathering on a Friday night, it was still fairly early and I didn't want to go home quite yet. I had a hankering for some quiet and some chocolate cake. I knew of a restaurant on Park Avenue that had it on their menu, so I called ahead and ordered a slice to go.

Chocolate cake in-tow, I decided to drive to the north end of the Avenue remembering some benches there near the Morse Museum. The lights were up for Christmastime and everything felt slow, lovely, and magical on this December night under those lights.

I enjoyed my dessert and sat thinking for a long while. The year held quite a few relational losses and redemption was on my mind. I, of course, had no solution about said redemption but I felt hope for it while I sat eating chocolate cake on my bench.

Time passed and a man strolled nearby. He ended up making his way over to me and asked if he could join me. He'd wondered what I was up to and I told him about my need for the quiet and the chocolate cake, of course. I learned that he owned the town homes across the street, and a lot more about his life and story.

For the longest time we sat there talking about this and that. Purpose, loss, tragedy, grief, and faith, all topics we covered blanketed by the dark and under the shimmer of Christmastime lights. At some point it started to sprinkle, then the rain came. We were mid-dialogue when he paused and said, "We're sitting in the rain, you know..."

"I know," was my simple reply.

"Okay, I just felt like I should say it."

We both just smiled a little and kept on talking. Two strangers on a bench in the rain. Hearing each other's stories, asking questions, being with each other for no other reason than the simple sake of presence.

Looking back, that evening conversation was very meaningful to me. We parted ways, but the experience has stuck with me. For whatever reason, the man's decision to say hello and invite himself to my little bench party was just what I needed that particular night. I think it may have been what he needed, too. I suppose there's something nice about the anonymity of an experience like this one but it really spoke to me about the power of being with another human, just with them. No agenda.

Why is it so hard for us to simply be with one another at times? I mean, I can think of ten reasons right now—I just wish more often I'd choose to be present with others like this stranger was with me. Instead of thinking of what our response will be, coming up with the solution to fix the problem being shared, or thinking about what we want to say next, we could just be with them.

Perhaps worse these days is the online space, where we're often making assumptions based on soundbites, assuming motives without knowing the actual person, or cancelling one another based on what we think we know or understand. The ugliness of accusation, slander, gossip, and information wars is growing while our honor of one another is virtually nonexistent. What we think we know ushers us into messy, messy places.

I wonder today what it would be like if we showed up like this man? What if we just asked to join another on the proverbial bench and we took time to learn about them? What if the discovery became a wonderful journey of knowing and being known?

The reality is, I didn't agree with every view he shared with me. I'd assume the same for him. But what was so special was the movement toward, the presence with, and the joy it sparked. I felt listened to, heard, seen, and known when I left our conversation. It renewed my hope in people after a year of losses.

If a conversation with a stranger could have results like that, what about those we actually do life with—family, friends, colleagues, acquaintances? How might we show up intentionally even for the stranger? I'm not suggesting everyone has to sit down with a random woman eating chocolate cake at night on a bench, nor that everyone has to accept a request from a stranger to share said bench. But what would it be like to have an openness to see another and care in our hearts to know them even just a little bit?

Whatever the circumstance, our willingness to see one another and show up for one another—simply to be with—matters. That conversation mattered so much to me. And before it happened, I didn't even know I needed it.

If you've looked around the country for even a moment, like me you've probably noticed we're on the brink of a breaking point. I believe it can be a beautiful breaking if we let it because it's a breaking off of our collective pride. We have important decisions to make not only regarding how we will continue to treat those we love, share life with, and work with but we will have to decide if we're willing to move toward those who are different than we are and unknown to us—those who think differently, vote differently, and those who have another approach to solving the same problem.

What if we decided to be done with the labels? What if, with a clean heart and pure motive, we reached out to someone we have previously labeled to simply know them, as a person, a fellow human being? What if we would just sit with them? What if we took responsibility for the labels we assigned and we started apologizing for labeling folks? What could change inside of you or me if we'd do this intentionally and regularly?

I believe we would see deepening connection. I believe we'd create real solutions that were broad in their helpful effect. I believe we wouldn't have to keep saying how we're not unified because we'd be like, "Nope, I'm having dinner with _____ tomorrow." (AKA I'm doing my part to build and establish connection.)

We push off on government and "them" what is often ours to own. We buy into narratives the media presents to us and accept it as truth. I'm not saying those entities or people don't matter or don't have a place and an influence. I simply believe in so many ways, we give them more place and more influence than needed. What if you and I just said enough is enough and started the hard work of building the bridges? I honestly believe all of the screaming heads in media and government might just eventually have to pull up a seat to see how it is that we're all working together and loving each other.

What we can say to them is, "Welcome to the table, my name is Jessica, and this is _____, and this is _____, and this is _____ … Tell us a little about yourself."

Being with cultivates understanding, empathy, and hope. The next time you have a conversation and say your farewell (or see you in a few minutes because we live in the same house), I invite you to try something I've been practicing in my life ...

Regarding the person (or people you just engaged with), ask yourself:

1. What, generally, did I learn about the person and their life?

2. What did I learn about the way they think?

3. What did I learn about their story that might contribute to that?

4. What did I learn about the "why" behind the way they do things?

5. Was there anything I disagreed with, but could see their perspective on?

6. And if you didn't learn anything like the above, maybe ask yourself why.

Reminder: You might not agree with everything you hear, but you will know the person better by taking time to be with them. You might not like the person at the end of the day, but being an honorable person means we honor even those we don't like. You might be surprised how much more you'll notice about people and how your curiosity grows the more you practice being with them. I know that's been true for me.

PRACTICE 10

The Power of Telling the Truth

Walking into one of my favorite retailers, I put on my mask (hello, 2020) and quickly headed toward the checkout area. The woman behind the counter greeted me and I proceeded to share how I'd visited a few weeks back, purchased three items and had later noticed I was only charged for two. I apologized for taking so long to return to the store (my life at times = a procrastination station) and told her I wanted to pay for the shirt. Her shock was evident.

"Wowww, thank you for coming back in. That's so nice of you," she said.

"Oh, not at all, it's the right thing to do," I offered.

As the interaction unfolded, I found myself feeling surprised by her surprise. What sort of a world do we live in these days where this is an uncommon occurrence, one worthy of this sort of a dialogue? She even gave me a discount on the shirt, by the way. Honesty has its rewards?

We finished our business and wished one another well. I left glancing at the sweaters but telling myself no way (real life). Then I ruminated on the interaction all the way home.

I view little moments like this in my life as tests. When minor items make their way onto my radar and I find I have a decision to make, the significance of the smallness is not lost on me. In fact, the smallness shows me the significance. Who would have noticed if I hadn't returned to pay for the shirt? Inventory would have revealed the loss. The store may have recorded it as lost or even shoplifting theft and recouped it. No one would be harmed, right? In fact, I might be preventing the sales staff person who missed ringing it up from getting in trouble. That's a good deed, isn't it? I promise I thought about all of these options. Nonetheless, once I knew, I had to make it right.

For the record, I don't always tell the truth or do the completely honest thing. Are you shocked? I know. It'll be okay. In all seriousness, I wish I did! I've had to process many regrets over the times I haven't told the truth. Practice, remember? But these days when I notice, like really notice, as in the case of the navy blue, soft as a baby lamb, long-sleeved shirt, I find myself frequented by the thought of it until I take care of the situation.

I find these tests come in the form of experiences like this one, or conversations where I tweak a detail and later consider, "Was that the truth?" Or the times when I feel like I need to make an excuse instead of just sharing my reality, and so on.

Do you have little areas of your life where you notice the line you're walking between what's true, what's honest, and what's not? Sometimes it feels annoying to notice, but then I feel gratitude because I know that truth breeds trust.

Over the years, I've been entrusted with information and access to people personally and to their companies, including financials. Information and access are valuable keys, handed over in trust. The thing is, if I'm someone who does not live in the truth and tell the truth, I ought not be trusted. Integrity says my words and my actions align. So you can see why I take this particular practice very seriously.

There are so many scams today. We scam each other relationally by using people to meet our needs. We scam each other by telling little white lies, tweaking details, or even hiding the particulars of what we're really going through to appear like we're more than or better than we are. We scam our employers by using the time they're paying us for other activities. We scam our employees in lack of credit for their work, appreciation, and even pay. We scam ourselves by not paying attention to the above realities and how we might be participating in them.

Some of the most untrustworthy people I've come across through the years are those who constantly lie to themselves. And the reality is, we all do this in some measure. Denial is one of our most well-established structures. You and I both live within its confines, in one way or another, each day. Meaning, we all have blind spots. We have ways in which we live and things that we say that don't align with us telling the truth about ourselves. But how can we tell the truth when we don't notice the gaps between who we say that we are and in practice, who we actually are?

My answer is two part: personal examination and people. When we employ this practice and resource, we can learn to tell the truth, come out of denial, and we can live with integrity in our lives. First, personal examination. The more aware we are about what we're believing, thinking, feeling, and how we're behaving, the better. When I recognized my outburst of anger-rage while playing *Settlers of Catan*, I was able to come out of denial and acknowledge the existence of that pattern in my life. Until I was willing to see it, nothing changed. Prior to that, I would have told you I had little to no problem with anger-rage and I would have totally believed myself. But it wasn't true. It was only when I saw and accepted the truth, that I could tell the truth.

Second, people. Who are your trusted advisors—those who know all, and I mean all, of your stuff? Does anyone know it all or have you parceled out pieces of knowing you between different folks? For me, I have several trusted advisors and the closest within that circle know all of my stuff. In fact, they probably know stuff that I don't yet know about myself. Not everyone has access to all of it, but a few do. Wisdom, friends. Not everyone gets access. But those who do are the friends who call me out, encourage me like crazy, continue to support me through the process of healing and transformation, and are trusted because they tell me the truth. And boy do I need it. I'll continue in my boldness and say ... you need it, too.

The reason I consider experiences like the now-paid-for-shirt as tests is because if I'm willing to notice the small, minute places in my life where I'm tempted to live outside of truth, outside of what is good and right, I feel some measure of comfort. Noticing is the first step, after all. In the noticing of what may seem small or insignificant, I am building and establishing a pattern to notice the larger and more significant places where I must tell the truth. If I don't practice in the small, who will I be and what will I do when I face something of utmost significance?

Remember how I talked about being entrusted with information and access? If I will not tell a retailer that I wasn't charged, how will I handle internal documents, balance sheets, confidential client meetings, professional mistakes I make, and beyond?

If I cannot tell the truth about myself and take personal responsibility for the way I show up in the world (beliefs, thoughts, emotions, behaviors, motives), making the appropriate changes in my life to deal as issues rise to the surface, how will I help others? In integrity, there's no way I can show up as a daughter, sister, friend, coach, or a consultant and powerfully help you if I'm not doing the work in my own life. It would be a facade. And that would be the true mask.

Questions for Reflection:

1. In what areas of my life am I not telling the truth?

2. What, to my knowledge, am I hiding, avoiding, distracting from, and/or living in denial of?

3. Why am I doing that?

4. What benefits do I gain by living this way?

5. What is being stolen from me by living this way?

6. Am I willing to do anything to change it?

Additional Considerations:

- If you came up with *nothing* as you asked yourself these questions, I invite you to go to a trusted advisor, a loved one or friend, who will tell you the truth, and ask them. I encourage you to be open to hearing their feedback. If you're not, it's a waste of time for you both.

- If you came up with *something* as you asked yourself these questions, I encourage you to go to your trusted advisor(s) and share what you uncovered. Ask them to speak into what you're noticing, invite additional feedback, and see how they might come alongside you as you move forward.

PRACTICE 11

The Power of Renewing Your Mind

If I was unexpectedly asked to stand up in a room and share some words on any personal growth topic today, without a doubt I would talk about beliefs. Our beliefs shape the way we see and experience life and if those beliefs aren't connected to truth, it will be extremely challenging to be resilient throughout the ups and downs of this life. This entire book is filled with examples of how beliefs shape everything in our lives.

We all have our own journey with our beliefs. The way I define beliefs is how we uniquely understand the world through agreements, which make up our mindset toward and about the world. The more I've grown and transformed over these years, and the more I've sat with clients and friends, I've identified an important thread that connects the many pieces of story I hear over and over, in session and out. That common thread is the agreements we make in childhood. Some are known to us, many are not. But the agreements, the beliefs we come to own as children, shape our whole lives and we build upon them over time unless the belief is confronted, and a new agreement is made.

Often we might remember something we went through, like I did with regard to the school performance I shared about in Practice 3. Or we might not recall making an agreement. After all, it wasn't until I looked back into that memory, and my experience with the teacher who was cruel, that I saw it clearly, "I never want to feel like this again." As a seven-year-old, I didn't know what a vow was, but I certainly made one. And throughout my life, up until the time I came into awareness of that vow, the consequences found me hedging my bets, choosing areas of competency over risk, and hiding behind both of those in an effort to avoid being shamed and feeling that way again.

In my recent history, I was reconnected with a trauma I endured and the accompanying memories that I had completely disassociated for over 30 years. There have been gaps in places in my story that I'd wondered about over the years, ways that I behaved that baffled me even after pursuing healing over many years, but I could never pinpoint the roots. It took time for the memories to resurface, I believe, because I had to heal enough, feel safe enough, for them to emerge and be dealt with at the right time. Even though it was shocking and deeply painful, once I reassociated, so many pieces of my story came into focus—things that didn't make sense before, now did. It was only then that I could confront the false beliefs I carried as a result of that trauma and replace them with the truth. As I have walked in this process, my mind has been renewed. And I see myself and the world differently, to a dramatic degree.

Confronting beliefs that are not serving us is powerful because when we do, we literally find freedom. When I realized I was living from that agreement "I never want to feel like this again," I had the opportunity to make a new decision. While it wouldn't feel great to be shamed again, what I have come to understand involves a few new thoughts and agreements I've made in the process:

- I don't know what was going on in that teacher's life that day, but I do forgive her for being cruel to me. I will not carry her cruelty with me any longer. I bless her and those she loves.

- I break agreement with the vow that "I never want to feel like this again" and I break agreement with all of the ways I put that agreement into practice by hedging my bets, hanging my hat on my competencies, and withdrawing from risk.

- I agree to press forward into new opportunities and through challenges, even if shame comes toward me in the process. I will put myself out there. I will make my attempt to the best of my ability. I will not fear shame or the feelings associated with shame any longer. Shame, you have no grip on me!

- I agree with God and with what He showed me from His perspective in my memory. He had a different role for me to play. I am fearfully and wonderfully made. His plans are so good and filled with joy, hope, and life. I embrace His plans and will see my experience through His lenses. I will initiate encouragement and spread it to those I meet, seeing what is so very special about each person, and I will call out what I discover in them.

Renewing our mind means we take the additional steps to end agreements with what isn't true and then fill that space with what is true. As our minds change, our lives change, because our emotions stem from our thoughts and our behaviors stem from our emotions. Can you see how these new agreements have completely shifted my trajectory for moving forward?

It would be shortsighted of me if I didn't share that this process takes a lot of intentionality and practice. Our ability to live with a renewed mind first means that we have a standard, a measure, of truth that we can renew our minds by—without this unshakeable, immovable standard, it would be quite difficult to practice the truth. Second, our ability to live with a renewed mind is connected to self-examination, personal responsibility, and humility. We must consistently be willing to dig in and notice, practice, and adjust course when we find ourselves spinning out in a direction that isn't bringing life to us or those in our path. For me, the practice of renewing my mind is paramount and ongoing. The investment is worth it, though. Some clients and friends have shared a discouragement that can accompany any ongoing practice like this, "When will I stop finding things?" My answer, "Probably never." At least not in this lifetime.

If that feels discouraging to you, I get it. But these days, my belief around this process is this: I'll gain a new layer of freedom! Genuinely, I'm motivated by each new step forward that I take by uncovering and dealing with an agreement that isn't leading me into the fullness of life because freedom is amazing. And I'm not always going out looking for this stuff, I find it naturally comes up in real life. Like when I blew up during the game with my family. I had to look no further than what I was experiencing in that moment to see that I had some work to do.

Living with a renewed mind is powerful because it ensures we stay in truth. When we stay in truth, we become unshakeable, resilient people. No matter what comes up in life, we don't go over the edge. It doesn't mean we don't experience highs and lows; it means we master our thoughts, emotions, and behaviors by maintaining our alignment with the truth.

I don't know about you, but in this world our ours, "truth" feels like it's constantly changing which really tells us it's not truth at all. Facts and truth aren't the same thing. Opinion and truth aren't the same thing. Perception and truth aren't the same thing. We must renew our minds by the truth. If we don't know what that is, or have a measure or standard for truth, consider that place of not knowing as an opportunity to seek it out. It's a beautiful endeavor. And in these years of pilgrimage, I've come to understand and embrace that truth has a name: Jesus. If you'd ever want to talk about Him, I'm here.

Twice a year, I offer an online course, Breakthrough Beliefs, to walk you through the process I use to do what I've shared in this chapter step-by-step. That way, you have a clear path forward to identify and confront the agreements you've made, deal with the roots of where they've come from, and change them in order to walk in more freedom. That resource is available to you if you'd like to go deeper. I'd be honored to help you in any way I can. (See page 81.)

Questions for Reflection:

1. Am I aware of any beliefs I hold today that aren't serving me?

2. If so, what are they?

3. Consider for a moment: Are there any agreements behind those beliefs?

4. Where did they come from?

5. How would I define the standard of truth that I apply when confronting ongoing beliefs or agreements in my life?

6. Does that standard shift or waver?

7. If so, how do I remain resilient through the ups and downs of my life?

PRACTICE 12

The Power of Generosity

Standing in line waiting for my turn with the teller, a quick thought came to my mind, *Get $10 cash out.* This is not an unusual occurrence for me, so when I walked up to the window, I made my deposit and requested the cash. Why $10? I was soon to find out. See, the Lord often speaks to me through these little prompts and it's like a nudge in the "prepare yourself, we're about to adventure together into something" kind of direction. Feeling a bit on alert, I left the building and noticed on the sidewalk, just north of the bank's parking lot, a woman in workout gear was taking a walk.

I hear, *Give her the cash.*

Too easy, I thought. *I'm only noticing her because of all of that.*

I walk to my car, start the engine, and consider how, just maybe, easy is the point. When I pulled out from the parking lot, sure enough, she was still there, straight ahead about a block east. I thought, *Why don't you just go with it ... It feels odd, but you have no idea what's happening in her life and you're making assumptions.*

I wasn't trying to stalk this woman, but I was afraid that it might appear that way if I slowly drove next to her on the street. I quickly came up with a plan, deciding to drive ahead of her, park, and exit my car to catch her on foot.

Have I mentioned that my life is an ongoing adventure like this? Because it really is. I do it. I park, jump out, and sort of wave her down.

"Hi, excuse me… I'm Jessica and this might sound very strange, but I wonder if you will allow me to gift you this cash?"

Meanwhile, she's pulling out her earbuds, trying to sort out what's happening, and responds, "Um, I mean, do I look like I need it? You don't have to do that …" in a matter-of-fact, not sure if she ought to be offended or confused, sort of tone.

I smile, "Oh no, it's not like that. It's that I was at the bank and felt like I needed to get it out to give someone, then I saw you and felt like the Lord really wanted me to give it to you … I think He wants you to know that you're on His mind today and that He loves you."

I handed her the money and she hugged me tightly and began to cry. "This makes things better today … "

"Would it be okay if I prayed for you?" I asked.

She nodded and we grabbed hands and took a moment to pray right there on the sidewalk. I blessed her into experiencing the love of Jesus that day and in my mind, I kept seeing coffee and said, "I don't know if you even drink coffee, but I really feel like the Lord wants you to treat yourself to something today that will be sweet and meaningful to you."

She said, "I'm totally going to get a coffee!" We both smiled big, then hugged again before we parted, teary from the sweetness of the interaction.

Who knew all of that was going to happen? Not me. I was worried about stalking a stranger.

Generosity comes in so many forms. Was it the idea for the cash? Was it her willingness to stop when a stranger was flagging her down on the sidewalk? Was it the $10 itself? Was it her willingness to vulnerably share? Was it the offer of prayer? Was it God's willingness to speak directly to her about how she mattered to Him? Was it her ability to receive? Was it the time spent together on that sidewalk?

I propose to you that generosity was threaded throughout this encounter and I'm just so very glad I didn't miss out on it. One of the greatest privileges that we have in this life is to demonstrate generosity to others. This is a lesson I hope I never depart from for all of my days.

When I get to be part, be "in" on something like the story I shared, it feels both thrilling and a little nerve-wracking (honesty!) all wrapped up into one. I tend to like to know the plan and His plan is typically, "Follow Me!" Then we're off.

But the other sweetness comes when we're the ones receiving. I believe we cannot be truly generous with others unless we're also good recipients of generosity ourselves. I was on the receiving end by being included in this story that day and she was on the receiving end of His loving gesture toward her. There is humility wrapped up in receiving and it's just so good for us.

If you've ever been on the receiving end of someone else's time, talents, and/or resources you probably know what I mean. I could write an entire book about the ways I have received from others and how those tangible demonstrations have shaped my life because the truth is, I've been that woman on the sidewalk on many a day. I've been at my end and have needed others to show up for me, see me, and help me.

There have been times I've shown up at my house to find a package of goodies, a plant, even a full-blown dinner on my doorstep. There was also a time when an entire sectional sofa showed up in my living room because of love and care. There have been times when a friend cleared her schedule to day-trip to the coast with me in the midst of heartache, and other friends got the tickets, brought me the outfit choices, picked me up, delivered me to the event and home again in a crazy work season when I couldn't take on one more thing. I've been profoundly moved by the love and generosity of those who supported my first book, journeyed with me for 14 years in faith-based non-profit work, cheered me on as I launched my companies, sent me coffee money for fun, and those who sneakily, but in the best sneaky way, filled in the gaps financially when *every single thing* dried up and I was living in panic.

I cannot say enough about them nor does this share even a part of a percent of it all. I've marveled by the way the Lord has shown His love for me through the generosity of others. It has changed me. And its motivated me into action.

To be truly generous means we're taking note. Note of our surroundings, note of people, note of needs, note of what could be even better, and even note of those little inklings we have like, "Maybe I should …" Being tuned-in positions us to live generously each and every day. When generosity isn't attached to anything else (like ulterior motives), it's just the most loving, life-giving practice.

When we share what we have with another and when we receive what another has to share, it has a way of righting wrongs, creating pathways for better, and ushering in new beginnings. Sharing cultivates connection, but I believe it cannot be coerced. We can do many things from a place of duty and some of that is right and good. Generosity, however, is a heart-driven practice. If it's not in our hearts, there will be no lasting impact, no deeper connection. We'll get a pat on the back for doing our duty and it'll end there.

But if our heart's desire is for connection and for wholeness and to help, we will demonstrate that desire in practical ways. And we'll do it with joy because we've actually tapped into a greater reality. When we pair our heart momentum with what we've noticed, powerful things can happen.

After all, what's $10? Certainly, it can meet a physical need briefly. If that's all it is, okay. That's good and has merit.

But what is $10 paired with care and intentionality, paired with encouragement, and some hope for the road? That money takes on a whole new form because money is just a tool, after all. Through generosity, we have the opportunity to bring meaning to what we're sharing. We get to write and live a better story as we do.

Becoming a generous person is powerful because it means we have skin in the game. We take our notes and we begin to act. So often these days, we pass our responsibilities off to other people or even to the government. "Let them help," we say. But instead, let's ask, "how are you and I to help?" What direct relationship can we cultivate where we can share what we have and make a difference right now?

In the process of building my companies, I've given a great deal of thought to what generosity means, what it looks like, what forms it takes, and how to implement the ideas well. I cannot afford to wait on others to take care of what I'm noticing each and every day. If I'm noticing, I have a part to play in creating the solutions. Each case is different, of course. I won't practice generosity in the same ways across the board. And I'm not waiting for that "someday" when I'll be able to _____. I'm doing what I can with what I have right now and dreaming about the ways I'll get to practice generosity in my future, too.

Each and every one of us has some measure, something we can give right now. Why wait? Why not take personal responsibility and determine the outworking of generosity with what you have, what you're noticing, and what stirs your heart right now?

Sometimes it is money, sometimes it's time, sometimes it's your talent (e.g. your ability to train and equip someone in your area of knowledge or expertise), sometimes it's your willingness to sit and be with, to listen, and offer feedback, and sometimes ... You fill in the blank. We have SO MUCH opportunity to give, if only we'd start noticing and taking action. Won't you join me?

Live in the power of generosity:

1. What am I noticing about—

    a) My surroundings

    b) People

    c) Needs

d) Things that could be improved

e) What I feel or think about, "Maybe I should ... "

2. What might I give in the next few months to cultivate meaningful connection and provide practical help in one or two of those areas?

3. Does that include my time, talents, resources, and/or other?

4. How will I practically take steps to act? What is step one? Step two? Step three? Etc.

5. Who can help? Is there someone else who has also noticed what I've been noticing? What might we do together better than we can do independently?

6. When will I get started? Literally, put it on your calendar and take action.

JESSICA BOTT

Keep Standing

This book was birthed from a series I created on social media during the late summer through the end of 2020. I began noticing how we were treating one another throughout the pandemic, the pursuit of racial justice and reconciliation, and of course, the US national election cycle. There was also light shed on the horrors of human trafficking and on those who have and continue to back, participate in, and expand the evil practice. What I saw, heard, and read deeply grieved me.

In a time we call "unprecedented," I've wondered what it could mean to approach all of these realities in a genuinely unprecedented way. After all, our opportunity to create and cultivate connection, understanding, and solutions has never been greater as the problems we face have brutally laid us bare. We have been confronted, in the best way possible, with ourselves.

Our pride, sense of entitlement, security, and health (spiritual, mental, emotional, physical, and yes, financial) have been challenged. We've been able to see the partnerships we've made with fear, comfort, slander, greed, shame, control, gossip, guilt, anxiety, and addiction, to name a few. And we've been given a gift—time to evaluate and navigate who were are in the here and now, who we will become as we take stock of how we're showing up in the world and make new decisions, and how we will choose to engage one another in the days, months, and years to come.

Freedom is a term we throw around quite loosely these days without perhaps understanding the profound nature of the gift. Will each of us employ our freedom to harm or help? Will we spend our best waking hours, or even our "free time," commenting upon and highlighting the perceived or actual failure of others, or will we employ our freedom to dig deep into our own lives to confront the ugly, guilty, contributing sources within our own character that add to what we all face today? Nothing changes if you and I do not change, after all. We can push responsibility off onto the "them," instead of looking at ourselves, but we will find ourselves in this same position time and again if this is the path we choose to walk in.

COVID-19 will pass. Other diseases, epidemics, and pandemics will come. In many regards, I believe we've lost sight of this fact in the current season. Fearmongering and its propaganda are at an all-time high. This is not the first challenge we've faced of the sort and it will not be the last, though profit and control-driven narratives keep us duped into division as we continue to participate in all of the finger-pointing. We can stop choosing the easy way out by instead deciding to roll up our sleeves and come together, especially in our differences. There are so many groups of people to consider. The sick, the isolated, the depressed, the elderly, the at-risk, and the healthy. Somehow, either we cannot or we're "not allowed" to hold them all in tandem together. Why is this? I believe it's critical for us to ask these larger questions and seek transformation at the root.

Injustice will remain until it's destroyed for good on a Day to come. Because sin exists, our propensity to live out our brokenness ensures that injustice will continue to be an enduring reality in this world of ours. So, it comes to this: what will we do about injustice in our time? This is what matters. But for now, we will always face it in one way or another. I don't say this to diminish what is and the work we must do in love and service of one another.

Rather, I speak this knowing that decades ago, my own grandparents faced profound injustice and trauma at the hands of both Hitler and Stalin and found a way in their hearts to forgive, to move forward, and to create a better life for themselves and their children. We have the same task ahead of us now.

But will we lay down our resentment, our hatred, our rage, our bitterness, and pick up genuine relationship with one another? How will we work together to design and establish better connecting points, systems, and even laws that ensure life, liberty, and happiness for all to the best of our ability? It's much simpler to point out the problems than to get around a table to create solutions. Part of the trouble is that we hold onto unforgiveness and resentment. Another part of the trouble is that when we do come around the table, we care about who wins. But instead, what if we cared deeply about doing what is good, what is right, what is integrous, and what is just? If we continue to choose our current way of being and relating, we will progress no further than we have to this day. Make no mistake, the trouble occurs on all "sides"—we all contribute to the problems we face. Yet, we are brilliant, gifted, and creative people. We can do better. We can be better. Let us!

If you and I will choose to practice what I've shared in these pages, I know our future will be quite hopeful. We have the privilege today to choose to stand. We can become steady, resilient, wise, humble, helpful, and loving people if only we choose it, if only we'll practice. Remember, standing requires something of us. It is an active posture that cultivates strength. It means, "I'm ready."

I know I'd simply be the most satisfied and grateful human if, at the end of my life, those who came to say their farewells could truthfully say of me, "Jessica stood."

What about you?

JESSICA BOTT

Acknowledgements

In a year with so many important moments, I am deeply grateful for/to:

Becky Thomton, editor-extraordinaire, you are simply the best. Thank you for receiving this idea and within days, making room in your life to move this project forward with me! If we ever wonder if we can get a book out at warp-speed, now we know. You are a tremendous collaborator and a genuinely great human. I am so grateful for the way you crush my run-ons sentences, repair my tenses, and offer me the most helpful insights into the big picture of what it is that is coming out of me. Plus, you generously process details I'm not sure that editors are intended to help with and that means so much. You and your family are wonderful. Thank you, thank you!

Emma Bush, thank you for taking on the graphic design aspect on such a tight deadline. I am grateful for your enthusiasm, creativity, and help in bringing this book to life! Your contribution has really encouraged and blessed me (and I hope many, many others)!

Leigh and Lisa, you both have been in the trenches with me throughout all 2020 has brought. Thank you for praying, listening, telling me the truth, offering sound wisdom, and for celebrating, championing, and grieving with me. I cannot adequately express how much it has meant that you have simply made the time to be with me.

I'm also grateful to both of your families for welcoming me in time and again. Both of you have offered me so much more than friendship—you have become family and I thank God for you.

Ford Taylor, you have made such a profound difference in my life. As I wrote this book, I reflected on how many of these practical applications I've grown in through your teaching and mentorship. Thank you for being someone committed to practicing what you believe in real life. And thank you for creating a community filled with others who do the same. I am better for knowing you and for being a part of Transformational Leadership. Thank you, thank you, thank you!

These friends, for being. Thank you, Amanda and Lander, Janae, Debbie Farah, Al, Em and Dave, Christine and Steve, Chele, Major, Jecca, Kristen and Sam, Shann, Nifer, Kate, Leela, Dana, Ash, Katie, Dena, Lisa R, and Casey.

My family (M, A, J, J, K, E)—what a year. There's a road on the path westward to our family home called Ramah. In Hebrew it means "the height" or "a high place of God." (Net Bible online) When I crossed over it this year, rain poured down and a rainbow marked out the rest of my drive ahead in the distance. Looking back, it feels so meaningful as I consider all that has transpired. Thank you for being with me, for seeing me, for learning to know me in new ways as we've traversed these days and spent time together and journeyed into healing from past traumas. Thank you for allowing me the opportunity to see and learn about you with new eyes, too. Thank you for *Settlers* and helping me to grow better into who I actually am. Thanks for a lot of laughs and a ton of deep conversations. I feel bolstered and encouraged by you. I feel overwhelmed by and grateful for all you've given to me in this extended season. I will continue to carry your tangible care and presence into all that's ahead. I will never forget it. Never ever. I love you.

Additional Resources

As a thank you for purchasing this book, **we're honored to send you a free gift**, *Practice Cards*, a tool designed to help you apply this content in daily life. Get your downloadable set by visiting:

www.jessicabott.com/practicecards

For a deeper dive into the 12 practices shared in this book, order your copy of the ***How to be a Better Human Workbook*** by visiting:

www.jessicabott.com/books

Breakthrough Beliefs is an online, self-paced course offered twice annually. You can learn more by visiting:

www.jessicabott.com/courses

ABOUT THE AUTHOR

Jessica Bott is a purpose-focused catalyst, dedicated to helping individuals and organizations identify and navigate change in health. By accelerating opportunities for transformation through a solutions-based approach, she develops clear plans that move people and organizations forward. Jessica passionately pursues understanding related to the root causes in order to resolve systematic issues. She is a business consultant, leadership coach, author, and speaker. Jessica is based in Orlando, Florida.